I hope you enjoy this journal and make sure to visit PearlHarmon.com

COPYRIGHT © 2022 BY PEARL HARMON

ALL RIGHTS RESERVED WORLDWIDE. THIS PRODUCT IS PROTECTED UNDER INTERNATIONAL AND NATIONAL COPYRIGHT LAWS IF YOU HAVE QUESTIONS PLEASE EMAIL PEARL@PEARLHARMON.COM

MOMENTS WITH MOM

A Legacy Journal
I chose to remember & capture moments

THIS JOURNAL BELONGS TO:

_____

DATE:

_____

PEARLHARMON.COM | © 2022 PEARL HARMON

Hi There,

Welcome to *Moments with Mom*. This journal is dedicated to my mother Lottie Bernice Carter Harmon and all who serve in the role of a mother. When mom transitioned I was left with a tremendous void. I soon realized that looking at photos/videos, cooking some of her favorite recipes, listening to a song, or writing gave me comfort and allowed me to feel her presence.

As you go about your daily life it is important to pause and capture moments, that you experienced or are experiencing with the mother figure in your life. Whether you are a parent looking to leave a legacy for your child or a child archiving memories, this journal is designed to serve as a cherished keepsake of memories, photos, words of wisdom, recipes, etc to help you preserve those treasures. Visit this journal often, and seek support from a licensed personnel if needed.

Love & Legacy,

Pearl Harmon

PEARLHARMON.COM | © 2022 PEARL HARMON

My Moments & Memories

Mindset

Develop a mindset to support you in capturing moments with mom. Create a plan and write your intentions below.

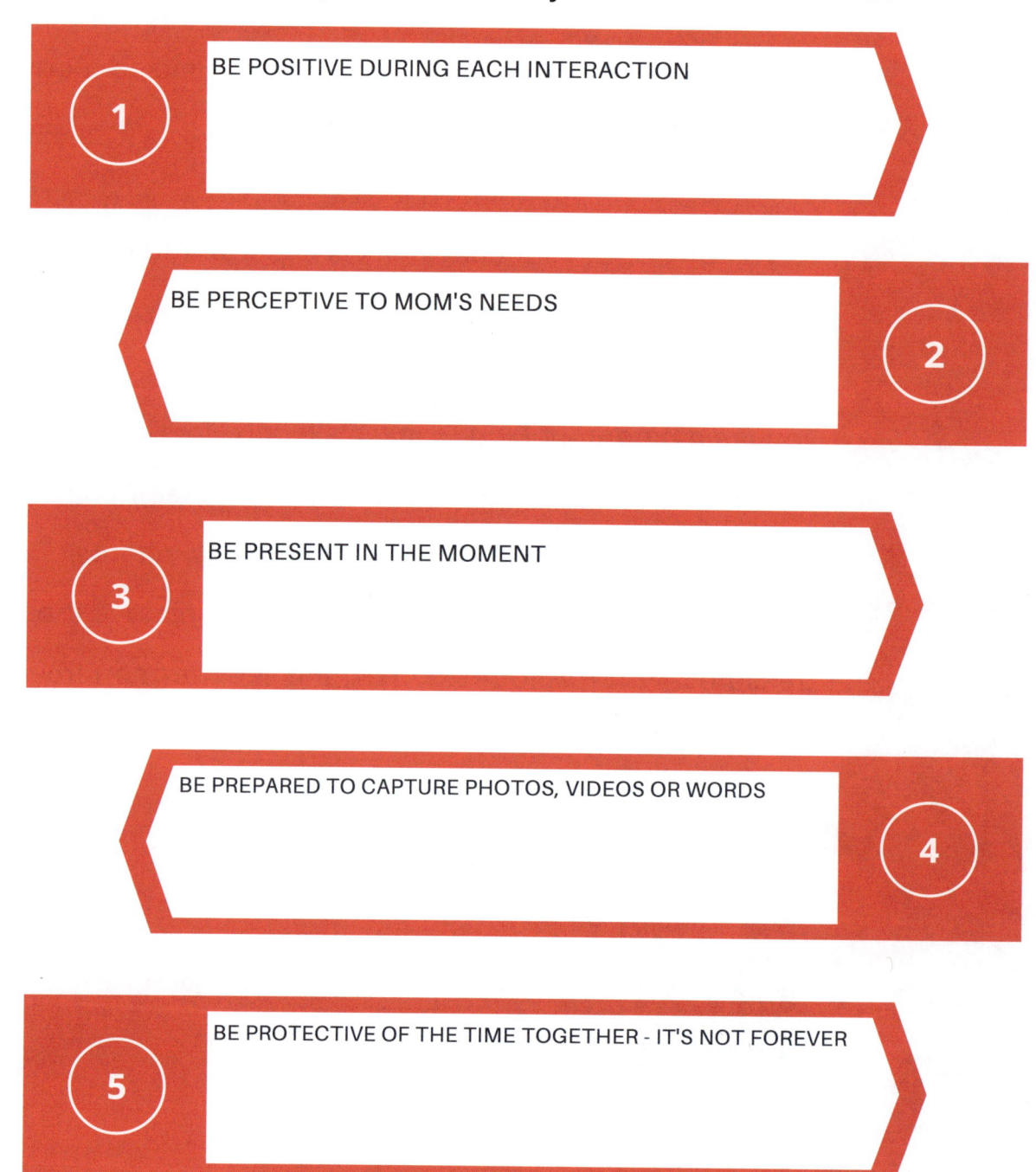

1. BE POSITIVE DURING EACH INTERACTION

2. BE PERCEPTIVE TO MOM'S NEEDS

3. BE PRESENT IN THE MOMENT

4. BE PREPARED TO CAPTURE PHOTOS, VIDEOS OR WORDS

5. BE PROTECTIVE OF THE TIME TOGETHER - IT'S NOT FOREVER

PEARLHARMON.COM | © 2022 PEARL HARMON

Just the Two of Us

PEARLHARMON.COM | © 2022 PEARL HARMON

My Personal Goal

By   /   /

I want to achieve

> **IMPERFECTLY PERFECT**
>
> **IS why YOU are so**
>
> **PERFECTLY PERFECT!**
>
> PB

PEARLHARMON.COM | © 2022 PEARL HARMON

POSITIVE NEW HABITS

MAKE A LIST OF THE THINGS YOU ARE GOING TO REMOVE FROM YOUR LIFE IN THE FIRST COLUMN AND WHAT YOU ARE GOING TO DO MORE OF IN THE SECOND COLUMN

STOP DOING LIST: ✗   DO MORE OF: ✓

Believe in your voice

PEARLHARMON.COM | © 2022 PEARL HARMON

"

EMBRACE
your journey
RENEWAL AWAITS YOU

Pearl Harmon

My 8 Week Memory & Moment Tracker

I COMMIT TO THIS GOAL:

TO BE SUCCESSFUL IN LIFE YOU MUST COMMIT TO A SPECIFIC OUTCOME UNTIL YOU CROSS THE FINISH LINE. I BELIEVE IN YOU!

Date: My Reward:

	HABIT WEEKLY GOAL	S	M	T	W	T	F	S
W1								
W2								
W3								
W4								
W5								
W6								
W7								
W8								

Yay! It's 8 weeks since I started my new habit to capture moments and this is what I achieved.

PEARLHARMON.COM | © 2022 PEARL HARMON

POSITIVE PAUSE

EACH TIME YOU OPEN THIS JOURNAL FIND ONE POSITIVE WORD BELOW AND CIRCLE IT. THAT'S YOUR SPECIAL WORD FOR THE DAY.

```
E M P O W E R E D Q B C G P D A A M A Z I N G X T W R P
O L T B O C P E R F E C T C K W M P X C A R I N G E W B H
R H U W S U C C E S S F U L P W M Q L M I L L I O N A I R E
L U C K Y V T Y P X B E A U T I F U L Q K L D E G I V I N G A
V H J U W P B H A P P Y W X A M I L E S M I L I N G T W P A
R E A D Y T O F L Y B U V E W S M A R T P N J S R G E N I U S
Y Q J K O G R A T E F U L P W W N L R B E L I E V E I N M E W
R O O W E V O L V I N G Q J V B E M O N E Y M A G N E T P E
R T I B S U N S T O P P A B L E S C I W L I M I T L E S S X Z I E
I A M U N I Q U E B H D E O M R B R I L L I A N T P W N E Y L E
I W M G R P A I A M L O V E D W U V A P R O S P E R O U S Q M
```

TODAY'S POSITIVE WORD IS:

_____   _____   _____
_____   _____   _____
_____   _____   _____
_____   _____   _____
_____   _____   _____
_____   _____   _____

PEARLHARMON.COM | © 2022 PEARL HARMON

Moment or Memory Catcher

Write down events you want to remember.

PEARLHARMON.COM | © 2022 PEARL HARMON

I Remember

Our Moments or Memories

PEARLHARMON.COM | © 2022 PEARL HARMON

Moments

Recipe for

NAME OF DISH

FROM THE KITCHEN OF

INGREDIENTS

SERVES

PREP TIME

TOTAL TIME

OVEN TEMP

DIRECTIONS

Made with love

PEARLHARMON.COM | © 2022 PEARL HARMON

Magical Moments
Notes

CAPTURING MOMENTS

*Date*_____

INSTRUCTIONS: WHAT MOMENTS DO YOU WANT TO REMEMBER?

_____
_____
_____
_____
_____
_____
_____

*Date*_____

INSTRUCTIONS: WHAT MOMENTS DO YOU WANT TO REMEMBER?

_____
_____
_____
_____
_____
_____
_____

Moments & Memory

_____
_____
_____
_____
_____
_____
_____
_____
_____
_____
_____
_____
_____
_____
_____
_____
_____
_____
_____
_____

Cherish mom's favorite things: song, flower, recipe, prayer...

Magical Moment

PEARLHARMON.COM | © 2022 PEARL HARMON

MOMENTS IN REVIEW   /   /

2 THINGS THAT MADE ME REALLY HAPPY:

1. _____
2. _____

2 UNEXPECTED THINGS THAT HAPPENED:

1. _____
2. _____

2 BIG ACCOMPLISHMENTS THIS WEEK:

1. _____
2. _____

1 THING I AM SUPER GRATEFUL FOR THIS WEEK:

1. _____

MY #1 GOAL FOR THE NEXT 7 DAYS:

1. _____

What will I tell my future self.......

> "Each moment creates memories that can impact lives for generations.
> — Pearl Harmon

PEARLHARMON.COM | © 2022 PEARL HARMON

Surrounded by Love

PEARLHARMON.COM | © 2022 PEARL HARMON

My Favorite Affirmations

> I will journey wherever my heart leads me.
> Pearl Harmon

Favorite Sayings

Write a quote, poem or draw

I Remember

Our Moments or Milestones

Moments

Notes

Recipe for

FROM THE KITCHEN OF

NAME OF DISH

SERVES

PREP TIME

TOTAL TIME

OVEN TEMP

INGREDIENTS

DIRECTIONS

Magical Moments Notes

CAPTURING MOMENTS

*Date*_____

INSTRUCTIONS: WHAT MOMENTS DO YOU WANT TO REMEMBER?

_____
_____
_____
_____
_____
_____
_____

*Date*_____

INSTRUCTIONS: WHAT MOMENTS DO YOU WANT TO REMEMBER?

_____
_____
_____
_____
_____
_____
_____

Moments & Memory

Cherish mom's favorite things: song, flower, recipe, prayer...

Magical Moment

PEARLHARMON.COM | © 2022 PEARL HARMON

MOMENTS IN REVIEW   / /

2 THINGS THAT MADE ME REALLY HAPPY:

1. _____
2. _____

2 UNEXPECTED THINGS THAT HAPPENED:

1. _____
2. _____

2 BIG ACCOMPLISHMENTS THIS WEEK:

1. _____
2. _____

1 THING I AM SUPER GRATEFUL FOR THIS WEEK:

1. _____

MY #1 GOAL FOR THE NEXT 7 DAYS:

1. _____

What will I tell my future self.......

> Mothers are named through Love

Pearl Harmon

PEARLHARMON.COM | © 2022 PEARL HARMON

Surrounded by Love

PEARLHARMON.COM | © 2022 PEARL HARMON

My Favorite Affirmations

> I will journey wherever my heart leads me.
> Pearl Harmon

Favorite Sayings

Favorite Songs or Music

I Remember

Our Moments

PEARLHARMON.COM | © 2022 PEARL HARMON

Our Moments
Notes

Recipe for

FROM THE KITCHEN OF

SERVES

PREP TIME

TOTAL TIME

OVEN TEMP

NAME OF DISH

INGREDIENTS

DIRECTIONS

made with love

Magical Moments Notes

CAPTURING MOMENTS

Date _____

INSTRUCTIONS: WHAT MOMENTS DO YOU WANT TO REMEMBER?

_____
_____
_____
_____
_____
_____
_____

Date _____

INSTRUCTIONS: WHAT MOMENTS DO YOU WANT TO REMEMBER?

_____
_____
_____
_____
_____
_____
_____

Moments & Memory

_____
_____
_____
_____
_____
_____
_____
_____
_____
_____
_____
_____
_____
_____
_____
_____
_____
_____
_____

Cherish mom's favorite things: song, flower, recipe, prayer...

Magical Moment

_____
_____
_____
_____

PEARLHARMON.COM | © 2022 PEARL HARMON

MOMENTS IN REVIEW   /   /

2 THINGS THAT MADE ME REALLY HAPPY:

1 _____
2 _____

2 UNEXPECTED THINGS THAT HAPPENED:

1 _____
2 _____

2 BIG ACCOMPLISHMENTS THIS WEEK:

1 _____
2 _____

1 THING I AM SUPER GRATEFUL FOR THIS WEEK:

1 _____

MY #1 GOAL FOR THE NEXT 7 DAYS:

1 _____

What will I tell my future self.......

> "You didn't know it but I was Destined to be your Child.

— Pearl Harmon

Surrounded by Love

PEARLHARMON.COM | © 2022 PEARL HARMON

♥
Places we like to visit

I Remember

Our Moments

PEARLHARMON.COM | © 2022 PEARL HARMON

Moments Notes

Recipe for

NAME OF DISH

FROM THE KITCHEN OF

INGREDIENTS

SERVES

PREP TIME

TOTAL TIME

OVEN TEMP

DIRECTIONS

Magical Moments Notes

PEARLHARMON.COM | © 2022 PEARL HARMON

CAPTURING MOMENTS

Date _____

INSTRUCTIONS: WHAT MOMENTS DO YOU WANT TO REMEMBER?

_____
_____
_____
_____
_____
_____
_____

Date _____

INSTRUCTIONS: WHAT MOMENTS DO YOU WANT TO REMEMBER?

_____
_____
_____
_____
_____
_____
_____

Moments & Memory

_____
_____
_____
_____
_____
_____
_____
_____
_____
_____
_____
_____
_____
_____
_____
_____
_____
_____
_____
_____

Cherish mom's favorite things: song, flower, recipe, prayer...

Magical Moment

MOMENTS IN REVIEW   /   /

2 THINGS THAT MADE ME REALLY HAPPY:

1. _____
2. _____

2 UNEXPECTED THINGS THAT HAPPENED:

1. _____
2. _____

2 BIG ACCOMPLISHMENTS THIS WEEK:

1. _____
2. _____

1 THING I AM SUPER GRATEFUL FOR THIS WEEK:

1. _____

MY #1 GOAL FOR THE NEXT 7 DAYS :

1. _____

What will I tell my future self.......

> **Mothers Strive Until they Thrive**
>
> — Pearl Harmon

PEARLHARMON.COM | © 2022 PEARL HARMON

Surrounded by Love

Write a quote, poem or draw

I Remember

Our Moments

Moments with Others

Recipe for

FROM THE KITCHEN OF

SERVES

PREP TIME

TOTAL TIME

OVEN TEMP

NAME OF DISH

INGREDIENTS

DIRECTIONS

made with love

PEARLHARMON.COM | © 2022 PEARL HARMON

Magical Moments Notes

CAPTURING MOMENTS

Date _____

INSTRUCTIONS: WHAT MOMENTS DO YOU WANT TO REMEMBER?

_____
_____
_____
_____
_____
_____
_____
_____

Date _____

INSTRUCTIONS: WHAT MOMENTS DO YOU WANT TO REMEMBER?

_____
_____
_____
_____
_____
_____
_____
_____

PEARLHARMON.COM | © 2022 PEARL HARMON

Moments & Memory

Cherish mom's favorite things: song, flower, recipe, prayer...

Magical Moment

MOMENTS IN REVIEW   /   /

2 THINGS THAT MADE ME REALLY HAPPY:

1. _____
2. _____

2 UNEXPECTED THINGS THAT HAPPENED:

1. _____
2. _____

2 BIG ACCOMPLISHMENTS THIS WEEK:

1. _____
2. _____

1 THING I AM SUPER GRATEFUL FOR THIS WEEK:

1. _____

MY #1 GOAL FOR THE NEXT 3 DAYS :

1. _____

What will I tell my future self.......

"

A Mother's Heart Resides Outside of Her Body.

— Pearl Harmon

PEARLHARMON.COM | © 2022 PEARL HARMON

Surrounded by Love

PEARLHARMON.COM | © 2022 PEARL HARMON

Write a quote, poem or draw

I Remember

Our Moments

Our Moments

Recipe for

NAME OF DISH

FROM THE KITCHEN OF

INGREDIENTS

SERVES

PREP TIME

TOTAL TIME

OVEN TEMP

DIRECTIONS

made with love

PEARLHARMON.COM | © 2022 PEARL HARMON

Magical Moments
Notes

CAPTURING MOMENTS

Date_____

INSTRUCTIONS: WHAT MOMENTS DO YOU WANT TO REMEMBER?

_____
_____
_____
_____
_____
_____
_____

Date_____

INSTRUCTIONS: WHAT MOMENTS DO YOU WANT TO REMEMBER?

_____
_____
_____
_____
_____
_____
_____

Moments & Memory

Cherish mom's favorite things: song, flower, recipe, prayer...

PEARLHARMON.COM | © 2022 PEARL HARMON

Magical Moment

MOMENTS IN REVIEW   /   /

2 THINGS THAT MADE ME REALLY HAPPY:

1. _____
2. _____

2 UNEXPECTED THINGS THAT HAPPENED:

1. _____
2. _____

2 BIG ACCOMPLISHMENTS THIS WEEK:

1. _____
2. _____

1 THING I AM SUPER GRATEFUL FOR THIS WEEK:

1. _____

MY #1 GOAL FOR THE NEXT 7 DAYS:

1. _____

What will I tell my future self.......

> # My Child, Each Breath is Taken for You

— Pearl Harmon

PEARLHARMON.COM | © 2022 PEARL HARMON

Surrounded by Love

PEARLHARMON.COM | © 2022 PEARL HARMON

Write a quote, poem or draw

I Remember

PEARLHARMON.COM | © 2022 PEARL HARMON

Our Moments

PEARLHARMON.COM | © 2022 PEARL HARMON

Teachable Moments

Recipe for

NAME OF DISH

FROM THE KITCHEN OF

INGREDIENTS

SERVES

PREP TIME

TOTAL TIME

OVEN TEMP

DIRECTIONS

PEARLHARMON.COM | © 2022 PEARL HARMON

made with love

Magical Moments
Notes

CAPTURING MOMENTS

Date _____

INSTRUCTIONS: WHAT MOMENTS DO YOU WANT TO REMEMBER?

_____
_____
_____
_____
_____
_____
_____

Date _____

INSTRUCTIONS; WHAT MOMENTS DO YOU WANT TO REMEMBER?

_____
_____
_____
_____
_____
_____
_____

Moments & Memory

Cherish mom's favorite things: song, flower, recipe, prayer...

Magical Moment

MOMENTS IN REVIEW   /   /

2 THINGS THAT MADE ME REALLY HAPPY:

1. _____
2. _____

2 UNEXPECTED THINGS THAT HAPPENED:

1. _____
2. _____

2 BIG ACCOMPLISHMENTS THIS WEEK:

1. _____
2. _____

1 THING I AM SUPER GRATEFUL FOR THIS WEEK:

1. _____

MY #1 GOAL FOR THE NEXT 7 DAYS:

1. _____

What will I tell my future self.......

> "A Mother's Love Can be Unspoken & Complicated.

— Pearl Harmon

PEARLHARMON.COM | © 2022 PEARL HARMON

Surrounded by Love

PEARLHARMON.COM | © 2022 PEARL HARMON

Dear _____

Date _____

3 THINGS I'M GRATEFUL FOR

THANK YOU

Pearl

Celebrate yourself for dedicating time to capture your mother's legacy. I hope you enjoyed the time spent with your loved one or with their memory.

If you are interested in more journals, or need support navigating the care of an elderly loved one, visit PearlHarmon.com.

Let's Connect

https://instagram.com/PearlHarmonConsulting

https://facebook.com/PearlHarmonConsulting

https://www.linkedin.com/in/pearl-harmon-7b8b1a65/

https://PearlHarmon.com

https://www.amazon.com/author/dr.pearl_harmon-1211

PEARLHARMON.COM | © 2022 PEARL HARMON

Made in the USA
Columbia, SC
20 February 2025